FROM FARM TO YOU

Bread

Carol Jones

CHELSEA HOUSE
PUBLISHERS

A Haights Cross Communications Company

Philadelphia

This edition first published in 2003 in the United States of America by Chelsea House Publishers, a subsidiary of Haights Cross Communications.

Chelsea House Publishers
1974 Sproul Road, Suite 400
Broomall, PA 19008-0914

The Chelsea House world wide web address is www.chelseahouse.com

Library of Congress Cataloging-in-Publication Data Applied for.
ISBN 0-7910-7007-7

First published in 2002 by
MACMILLAN EDUCATION AUSTRALIA PTY LTD
627 Chapel Street, South Yarra, Australia, 3141

Edited by Anne McKenna
Text design by Judith Summerfeldt Grace
Cover design by Judith Summerfeldt Grace
Illustration on p. 18 by Pat Kermode, Purple Rabbit Productions

Printed in China

Acknowledgements
The author wishes to thank David, Keith and Garth of the Firebrand Bakery for their help with the writing of this book.

Cover photographs: Bread display and bread texture courtesy of Getty Images/Photodisc.

AKG: London/Erich Lessing, p. 5 (bottom); APL/Corbis © Gianni Dagli Orti, p. 6, © Archivo Iconographico, S.A., p. 7 (bottom), © Macduff Everton, p. 7 (top); Coo-ee Picture Library, p. 9 (bottom); Copper Leife/Craig Forsythe, pp. 20–7, [20 (bottom), 21 courtesy of Goodman Fielder, 20 (top), 22–5 courtesy of Tip Top Bakeries, 26–7 courtesy of Safeway], 28 (Turkey), 29 (Russia); Corbis Digital Stock, p. 28 (Italy); Getty Images/Tony Stone, pp. 4, 8 (bottom), FPG International, p. 18, Photodisc, pp. 3 (top left and right), 28–9 (map), 28 (Denmark, France and Egypt), 29 (USA and Mexico); Imageaddict, pp. 19 (bottom), 28 (England); Carol Jones, pp. 3 (bottom left and right), 10–15; Mary Evans Picture Library, p. 5 (top); Stockbyte, pp. 16–17, 19 (top), 20 (bottom).

Contents

The world of bread

Next time you visit a bakery or supermarket, take a look at the many shapes and sizes of bread on the shelves.

There are round loaves, rectangular loaves, braided loaves, sticks, rolls and flat breads, to name just a few. It is hard to believe that the three main ingredients in all these products are the same — flour, water and salt. In most raised or leavened breads, it is just **yeast** that has been added.

Bread is made with flour ground from cereal grains such as wheat, rye, corn, barley and oats. It can be raised or flat. It can be home-baked on a hot stone or produced by machine in a large factory.

Bread of some kind is eaten almost all over the world.

This Turkish boy is carrying a tray of flat bread.

The history of bread

Bread was first baked nearly 12,000 years ago in Neolithic times.

Very early hunter-gatherers in the **Middle East** probably harvested wild grains from native grasses. The grains were ground or crushed between stones. This coarse flour was mixed with water to make dough. Then lumps of dough were cooked on stones that had been heated in a fire.

Over time, people learned which grains grew well and could be stored best. They planted the grain and settled down to become farmers. More than 8,000 years ago, the Sumerian people of Iraq were **sowing** wheat. The Chinese were growing it 5,000 years ago.

Long ago, grain was crushed in a saddle quern by rolling a rubbing stone backwards and forwards over a base stone.

This sculpture from Ancient Greece shows four bakers kneading dough.

Firsts

The first breads were very coarse. Scientists have found skulls of Stone Age people that show how their teeth became worn and chipped from eating this gritty bread.

Early peoples from the Middle East, Asia, Africa and America, and possibly Australia's Aboriginal people used these grinding and cooking methods. But about 4,600 years ago, the ancient Egyptians discovered how to make leavened or raised bread — probably by accident.

Some bread dough was probably left outside for too long. Wild yeast **spores** settled in the dough and began to feed on the flour. The yeast gave off bubbles of gas as it fed and the bread began to expand with the gas. The Egyptians also invented an oven made from a clay cylinder.

Ancient Egyptian wall paintings more than 3,000 years old show wheat being harvested.

Strange but true!

Wheat grains that are thousands of years old have been found in the ruins of ancient Egypt. Nobody has tried making them into bread though!

The Romans learned bread making from the ancient Greeks, who learned it from the Egyptians. The Romans spread the word throughout their empire. In ancient Roman bakeries, grain was ground between two huge round stones. These millstones were turned by slaves or donkeys. Bread was baked in large brick ovens.

In Europe in the **Middle Ages**, millstones were powered by water or wind. Flour for very rich people was sifted through silk to make lighter, whiter flour. Large towns had bakers. But most country people still made bread at home and baked it on a flat iron plate called a griddle, which was covered with a pot.

This Mexican woman is making bread.

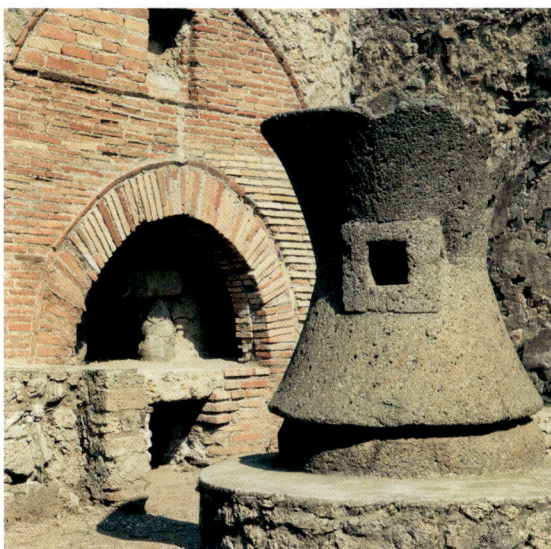

This Roman bakery from the town of Pompeii was covered by lava when the volcano Vesuvius erupted in 79 A.D. It was dug out in 1810.

Famous last words

In France in the 1700s, many people were hungry and angry about the high price of bread. They rose up against King Louis XVI. One false story tells that his queen, Marie Antoinette, did not care that the people could not afford to buy bread. The rumor says she insulted the poor by saying, 'Let them eat cake!' In truth, Marie never said this. The quote was recorded in a book written two years before Marie became queen, so it was most likely said by someone else.

Kinds of bread

There are three main kinds of bread: flat, yeast and quick breads.

1. Flat breads

Flat breads are usually made without yeast or any other rising agent. Flat breads are traditional in the Middle East, India and Central America. They can be made from corn, barley, millet, rice, wheat or rye. They can be cooked on an iron pan or griddle, such as Indian chapatti, or baked quickly in a very hot oven, such as Egyptian pita.

Tortillas are a flat bread from Mexico.

Preservation

Some flat breads, such as Jewish matzo, are cooked until crisp and light. If kept dry they can be stored like a cracker. Centuries ago, sailors ate dried bread called hardtack on long voyages. It was made from flour and water and baked until it was so hard it could keep for years. Unfortunately, on a damp ship, it was soon alive with insects called weevils!

Yeast makes bread rise.

2. Yeast breads

Some flours contain a **protein** called gluten. When this type of flour is mixed with water, the gluten makes the dough stretchy so that it can rise. Wheat flour and rye flour are used for making yeast breads because they have the most gluten.

Yeast is a single-celled living organism called a fungus. When yeast is added to the flour, salt and water mixture and left in a warm place, the yeast gives off gas that makes the bread rise. Then the dough is cooked.

Yeast breads can be baked in tins or shaped by hand. You can see the empty gas bubbles from the yeast when you cut a loaf of bread.

3. Quick breads

Quick breads take less time to make than yeast breads because they use baking powder or another rising agent. Quick breads rise in the oven, not before cooking. They can be baked in pans or shaped by hand. Muffins, corn bread, scones and Australian damper are all quick breads.

These Australian children are baking a bread called damper over hot coals.

How bread is made

Today, most bread is made in large factory bakeries by **automated** machines, but cities and towns often have smaller bakeries that still bake their bread the old-fashioned way.

The bakers shown here are making sourdough bread in a wood-fired oven. Bread has been baked this way since Roman times.

Ingredients

To make this sourdough bread, the bakers use the following ingredients:
- unbleached white flour, stone-milled wholewheat flour or stone-milled rye flour
- sea salt
- warm water
- yeast culture (leaven).

The bakers work on a large clean counter when hand-shaping the dough.

Scales for weighing the dough

Stacked shelves for proofing the bread

Tins for baking the bread

Tools and equipment

Many of the tools used by these bakers are similar to those used hundreds of years ago. Some of the tools these bakers use are:

- dough-mixing machine
- scales for weighing dough
- tins for holding bread
- cloths for folding around bread
- large plastic trays
- stacked racks or shelves
- wood-fired brick oven
- peel — a long-handled wooden tool with a flat paddle for lifting bread in and out of the oven.

Method

Mixing the dough

The night before baking, bakers add water and flour to a bucket of yeast culture (leaven). The mixture is left to **ferment** and grow overnight. Every day the bakers save a little of the yeast culture to use for the next day's baking. In this way, the bakers have used the same yeast culture for many years.

Early the next morning the bakers arrive. They measure the correct amounts of leaven, flour, salt and water into the dough mixer. The water temperature needs to be just right. In cold weather, the bakers use warmer water than in hot weather. On the hottest days they may even add ice to the water.

The bakers stop the machine during mixing to feel the dough. Bakers know from experience whether to add more water or flour to the mixture. After more mixing, the dough is lifted from the mixer. It is left on a clean counter for an hour for the yeast to do its work. This is called bulk proofing.

Checking the dough in the dough mixer

Bulk proofing the dough on a counter

Lighting the oven

The wood fire for the oven is also lit at this time. The bakers fire up the oven to make it twice as hot as they need it. They can check the temperature of the oven on the pyrometer, a special oven thermometer. Then they let it cool down to the right temperature for baking. The oven holds the heat inside. This is called radiant heat, which is heat that does not come directly from a flame. This radiant heat will bake the bread.

A wood-fired oven works by radiant heat.

Shaping the loaves

The bakers cut the dough into loaf-sized pieces and weigh them to make sure they are the correct size. Then the dough is hand-shaped and placed in greased tins, or rolled into long loaf shapes and placed between folds of thick cloth. The loaves are placed in racks and left in the warmth of the bakery to rise for three hours. This is the second proofing.

Shaping loaves by hand

13

Baking the bread

In a wood-fired oven, the first bread put in will be the last taken out. Therefore, loaves that take the longest to bake go in first. Loaves without tins sit directly on the brick floor of the oven. The bakers score, or cut, the tops of these loaves. Scoring helps the bread keep its shape and makes it crustier.

The baker scores the tops of the loaves.

Next, the tin loaves are placed in the oven, followed by the small loaves and then the rolls. About 200 loaves fit into the oven. Large loaves bake for 40 minutes. Rolls bake for 25 minutes.

In the oven the dough blooms. This means that the yeast gives off gas and the dough expands. When the temperature reaches 158 degrees Fahrenheit (70 degrees Celsius), the bread stops rising because the yeast dies.

The peel is used to place loaves in the oven.

Removing the bread from the oven

When the bread is done, the bakers remove the loaves from the oven with the peel. The color of the bread is checked. The bakers can tell if the loaves need to be left in the oven for another minute or two. Loaves are tipped out of their tins onto large plastic trays. The hand-shaped loaves are put directly onto the trays. All the bread is stacked neatly.

As each tray is filled, it is moved to a rack for cooling. The bakers work quickly to get all the bread out of the oven and stacked before it is overbaked.

Once the bread has cooled to a warm temperature, it is taken into the shop for sale.

Removing the baked loaves from the oven with a peel

Stacking the hand-shaped loaves in trays

The bread factory

Most of the bread we buy is made in large factory bakeries. These bakeries make different kinds of breads, including bread rolls, muffins and crumpets.

From farm to consumer

Follow the flowchart to see how wheat is grown, **processed**, made into bread in large bakeries and then transported to stores for sale to the **consumer.**

Read more about each stage of the bread-making process and how bread is marketed and sold on pages 18 to 27. Look for the flowchart symbols that represent each stage of the process.

Farming the wheat
Farmers grow wheat on fairly flat land that is not too wet or too dry. When the wheat is ripe, it is **harvested**.

Packaging the bread
Packaging materials may be made elsewhere and delivered to the **manufacturer**.
Most bread made at large factories is sliced and packaged in plastic bags.

Transport and storage
Packaged bread is loaded onto plastic **pallets** and transported to stores or sent to other companies such as fast-food outlets.

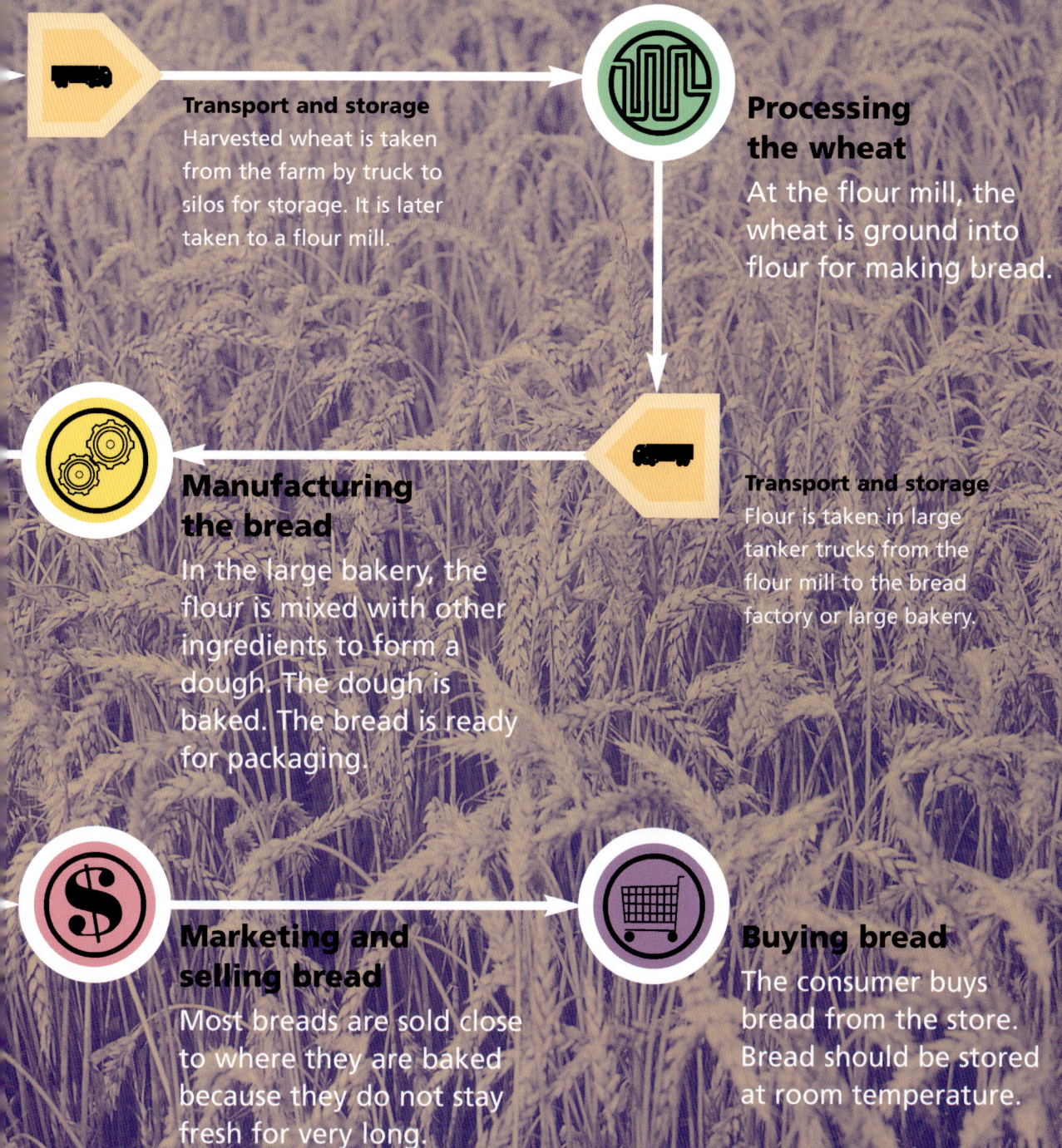

Transport and storage
Harvested wheat is taken from the farm by truck to silos for storage. It is later taken to a flour mill.

Processing the wheat
At the flour mill, the wheat is ground into flour for making bread.

Manufacturing the bread
In the large bakery, the flour is mixed with other ingredients to form a dough. The dough is baked. The bread is ready for packaging.

Transport and storage
Flour is taken in large tanker trucks from the flour mill to the bread factory or large bakery.

Marketing and selling bread
Most breads are sold close to where they are baked because they do not stay fresh for very long.

Buying bread
The consumer buys bread from the store. Bread should be stored at room temperature.

Farming the wheat

Wheat is grown on fairly flat land that is not too wet or too dry. Wheat farmers use machines for sowing and harvesting their crops.

Wheat can be planted at different times of the year. Farmers who live in mild climates grow winter wheat. They plant winter wheat in fall and harvest it in spring or summer. Farmers in cooler climates grow spring wheat. They plant spring wheat in spring and harvest it in summer. Spring wheat matures faster, but winter wheat produces more kernels.

Huge wheat crops are grown in the United States, Canada, India, Russia and France.

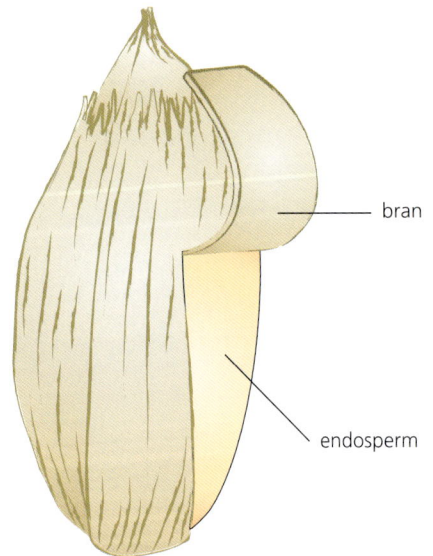

bran

endosperm

A grain of wheat

Transport and storage

After harvest, the wheat is taken by truck to a grain elevator near a railroad track. Trucks empty the wheat into large pits, then a conveyor belt carries the grain to the top of a large storage bin. The wheat must be kept dry and free of insects.

Farm machinery

Modern wheat farmers use many machines. A plow or cultivator prepares the soil for planting. A drill combines seed and **fertilizer** and drops them into **furrows**. These machines are pulled by tractors. Many farmers also use a boomspray to spray chemicals for weed and pest control. When the grain is ripe, a combine cuts the heads of the wheat and separates the grain from the **chaff**.

A modern combine at work

Silos for storing wheat

Farm workers

Farmers and farm hands

Truck drivers

Workers at the grain elevator

Railway workers

Conservation

Wheat takes **nutrients** from the soil. To replace these, some farmers rotate crops every year. After a field has grown wheat, the farmer might plant another crop such as corn or soybeans to put nutrients back into the soil, or leave the field unplanted for the season.

From the grain elevator, wheat is loaded into railroad cars and transported to a large grain terminal for shipping. There, different types of wheat may be blended for flour mills, or the grain may be inspected for shipping overseas.

Processing the wheat

At the flour mill, wheat for bread making is processed. This means it is graded, cleaned, blended, soaked, ground, sifted and ground again to make flour.

First, wheat is inspected and graded for quality before it is sorted into groups. Different wheats are used for different products. Several grades of wheat are usually blended to make different kinds of flour. Soft wheat is used for cookies and hard wheat is used for bread.

Grain is cleaned to remove any stones, dust and weed seeds. It is soaked in water for 10 to 20 hours. This toughens the outer **bran** layer to make it easier to separate, and softens the inner **endosperm**. Whole-wheat flour is made from both parts of the wheat kernel, but white flour is made using only the endosperm.

This machine cleans the wheat.

The wheat is blown through a chute into a waiting truck.

Transport and storage

Flour is stored in bags or bulk bins for three days. Then it is blown through a chute into a waiting truck. Trucks are totally sealed so that dust cannot get into the flour.

Sieving and crushing the wheat

The wheat is fed into grooved roller mills that rotate toward each other. The bran is broken away from the endosperm, which is crushed to make **semolina**. This is sieved and separated into bran and semolina by air blown through machines called plansifters. The semolina is crushed further in smooth roller mills and sifted again. This may happen up to 12 times before the semolina is fine enough for flour.

Wheat is crushed in roller mills.

Processing workers

Production-line workers

Engineers

Transport workers

Strange but true!

The grooves on old-fashioned stone mills were very important for breaking open the grain. After about 100 hours of milling, the grooves wore down and had to be repaired. It was the job of a traveling millwright to chip away at the stones. This could take 18 hours.

Trucks are weighed to measure the weight of the flour, which is then delivered to large bakeries.

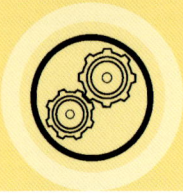

In large bakeries, bread making is fully automated. **Additives** and special methods are used to speed up proofing and keep bread fresher for longer.

Ingredients are weighed and prepared. Wet and dry ingredients are combined in the dough-mixing machine. In bread factories, the mixture is usually blended at high speed. This is called 'no time dough mixing'. It speeds up the working of the yeast.

A divider cuts the dough into pieces of the same weight and size. The pieces then enter the rounder — a cone-shaped revolving drum. The pieces of dough spiral up through the rounder being rolled and turned, coming out with a rounded shape.

The dough then rests in a special cabinet called a prover. Temperature and **humidity** are controlled, so that the yeast works quickly and efficiently.

A divider cuts the dough.

Transport and storage

After the flour arrives from the flour mill, it is stored in a silo. Liquid or cream yeast is stored in temperature-controlled stainless steel tanks. **Conveyor belts** are used to move the bread through the bakery.

Baking the bread

The dough is then moved to the ovens. The ovens are so large that loaves keep moving through. By the time they come out the other end they are baked. The loaves are removed from their tins by a depanner. The depanner uses suction caps to lift the bread from the tins. The bread then moves to the cooling area, where air flows over and around the loaves, cooling them to about 100 degrees Fahrenheit (38 degrees Celsius).

Bread moving to the cooling area

Bread moves into and through the ovens on a conveyor belt.

Manufacturing workers

Bakers

Production-line workers

Engineers

Chemists

Food technologists

Additives

As well as adding ingredients for flavor and taste, such as grains, fiber and fruit, large bakeries may put in some of the following:

- **emulsifiers** to make dough easier to mix and knead
- preservatives to keep the bread fresh longer and help stop mold from growing
- **vitamins** such as thiamine.

23

Packaging the bread

Most bread from large factories is sliced, packed in bags and transported to stores or directly to large consumers.

Once the bread is cool, it is taken to be sliced. A slicing machine is made up of many thin metal blades. The blades are spaced to cut the thickness of a slice. They slice each loaf in one movement.

When the loaves are sliced, a machine places them into thin plastic bags. Bags are stacked on a wire frame that contains hundreds of bags. Air is blown into the bags so the loaves can be put into them. They are then sealed and coded with a date.

The packaged loaves are stacked in crates ready to be loaded onto trucks.

A slicing machine at work

Transport and storage

Crates of bread are loaded onto trucks and delivered to supermarkets and small stores.

The bags are made by a packaging company. They are printed with the name of the bread and the manufacturer, a list of ingredients and nutritional information. This tells the consumer what is in the bread and how it might be good for them.

Bread packaging contains and protects the bread during transport and handling. It helps keep the bread fresh and gives consumers information about the bread and its maker.

Bread is placed into bags by a machine.

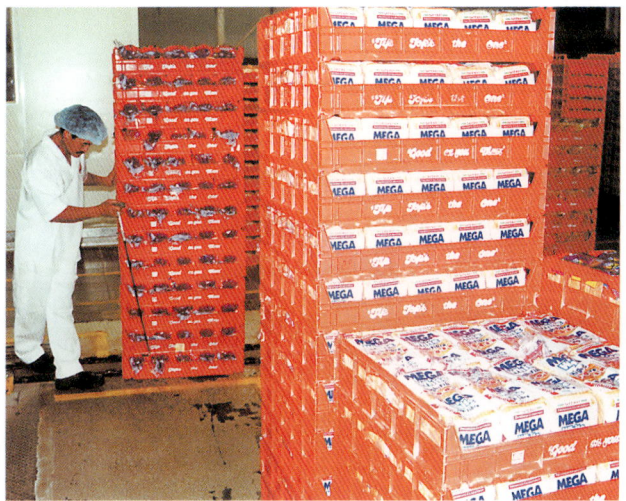

The packaged loaves are stacked in crates ready to be loaded onto trucks by forklifts.

Bread is also delivered directly to large organizations such as schools, hospitals and fast-food outlets.

Packaging plant workers
Production-line workers
Graphic designers
Transport workers

Marketing and selling bread

Most breads do not stay fresh for long and are sold close to where they are baked. Large bakeries use advertising to encourage consumers to buy their product.

Large baking companies need bakeries in more than one place. Most have city and regional bakeries. Workers from the baking companies, called merchandisers, visit stores to make sure that they are receiving the kinds and amounts of bread they need. Merchandisers also organize special displays and tastings to help advertise their company's products.

Large companies can also afford to advertise their products to a larger audience. They might place ads in magazines or on television. Some companies have their own websites to tell consumers about their products.

Stocking the shelves at the supermarket

Marketing and sales workers
Merchandisers
Shelf-fillers
Checkout operators
Bakers
Graphic designers
Copywriters

Many consumers buy their bread at supermarkets or small stores. Some people prefer to buy their bread where it is baked. They usually buy it from small bakeries. Because of this, some large supermarkets now have their own in-house bakeries producing breads, buns and cakes.

Bread is an important part of most people's daily diet. It can be eaten at any time of the day — as toast for breakfast, as a sandwich for lunch, with dips for a snack, or with soup or salad for dinner.

Some supermarkets have their own bakeries because consumers like to buy their bread where it is baked.

Home storage

Most bread goes directly onto the shelves for sale. At home, bread should be stored at room temperature. Bread can also be frozen for several weeks.

Bread around the world

In England, cottage loaves are a traditional bread.

Rye bread is popular in Denmark.

Turkish bread

French baguettes are long sticks of light, crusty white bread.

Italy is famous for inventing pizza — a flat bread with yeast.

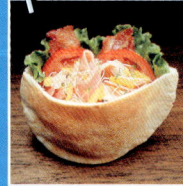

Egyptian pita is a flat wheat bread with a pocket inside.

Lebanese flat bread

Russia is known for its dark rye bread.

Hamburger buns from the United States have become popular around the world.

Mexican tortillas are flat breads made from corn flour. They can be wrapped around other foods.

Make your own bread rolls

Use this recipe to make crusty bread rolls at home with help from an adult.

Bread rolls

Ingredients

- 3 cups of bread-making flour
- 1 teaspoon of salt
- $1\frac{1}{4}$ cups of warm water
- 1 teaspoon of vegetable oil
- 2 teaspoons (1 package) of dried yeast
- 1 teaspoon of sugar

Equipment

- clean counter
- oven mitts
- 2 mixing bowls
- greased baking tray
- large plastic bag
- sieve
- cloth

Method

1. Sift the flour and salt together in a bowl.
2. Pour the water and oil into the other bowl and stir in the yeast and sugar until it is well mixed.
3. Make a well in the flour and pour in the liquid. Mix well to form a dough.
4. Place the dough on a clean counter sprinkled with flour. Fold it in half and gently press down. Keep doing this (kneading) until it becomes a bit sticky — about 5 minutes.
5. Make a ball with the dough, put it back in the bowl, cover with a cloth and leave it to rest for 15 minutes. This is the first proofing.
6. Divide the dough into 10 pieces, roll each into a ball and place on the baking tray.
7. Cover the tray with a plastic bag and leave it in a warm place for about 45 minutes. This is the second proofing.
8. Remove the bag and place the tray in a preheated 450 degree Fahrenheit oven for 10 to 15 minutes or until the rolls are golden.
9. Carefully remove the tray from the oven with oven mitts. Let the rolls cool before eating.

Glossary

additives   substances added to improve something

automated   machines that work with little human help

bran   the tough outer layer of the wheat grain

chaff   bits of straw left after wheat heads are separated from stalk

consumer   person who buys goods or services

conveyor belts   endless strips of material, such as rubber, on rollers used to move something

emulsifiers   salts that help one substance blend with another

endosperm   the white inner part of the wheat used to make white flour

ferment   to cause a chemical reaction that changes the nature of the food

fertilizer   a substance added to soil to help plants grow

food technologists   workers who scientifically test or treat food

furrows   shallow trenches

harvested   picked the crop

humidity   the amount of moisture in the air

manufacturer   person or company that makes goods

Middle Ages   period in Europe from 500 A.D. to 1500 A.D.

Middle East   area around eastern Mediterranean Sea, from Turkey to North Africa

nutrients   food substances that help us stay healthy

pallets   large trays

processed   treated in a special way

protein   important nutrient needed by people

semolina   a coarse flour

sowing   planting

spores   parts of a plant used to reproduce

vitamins   important nutrients needed by people

yeast   a fungus that ferments sugars as it reproduces

Index

641.8
JON

DATE DUE